Mdina

The silent city
RABAT - MOSTA

MILLER

Miller Distributors Limited
Miller House, Tarxien Road, Airport Way, Luqa Malta.
P.O. Box 25 Malta International Airport LQA 05
Telephone: 664488 Facsimile: 676799

CENTRO STAMPA EDITORIALE

PERSEUS

Index

Mdina 4
Main Gate 8
Magisterial Palace 10
Tower of the Standard 11
Cathedral Museum 12
Cathedral Church 23
Falzon Palace (Norman House) 30
Greeks' Gate 31
Villegaignon Street 31
Rabat 36
Museum of Roman Antiquities 37
St. Paul's Collegiate Church 42
St. Paul's Grotto 44
Museum of St. Paul's Church 46
St. Paul's Catacombs 47
St. Agatha's Church 48
Verdala 54
Dingli 56
Mosta 57
Plan 62

Text: John Azzopardi
Photographs: Archivio Plurigraf - Kevin Casha - Daniel Borg - Jonathan Beacom & Perfecta Advertising.

© Copyright
CASA EDITRICE PERSEUS - PLURIGRAF collection
Published and printed by Centro Stampa Editoriale, Sesto Fiorentino, (Fi).

Mdina

Mdina with its Mediaeval and Renaissance palaces, churches and fortifications and its narrow streets has a character of its own. It was the island's capital city until 1568, when the Knights of St. John after the bitter experience of the Great Siege of 1565, built the new city of Valletta.

Its present area covers only a third of Malta's older city, called by the Romans, like the island itself, Melita. That older city, whose origin is lost in the mist of antiquity, inhabited by the Greeks, the Romans and probably the Phoenicians, extended up to the centre of modern Rabat. In the Roman era and maybe earlier it was surrounded by a ditch, parts of which have been preserved behind St. Paul's Collegiate Church, Rabat, just outside the walls and hence referred to, as in Rome, St. Paul Outside the Walls. Presumably for reasons of defence, the Arabs reduced its size to its present outline and dug the moat which is still in existence. They also changed the name, calling the town simply MDINA - the city - and the newly formed suburb RABAT - the environs. Both names are still in common use.

The Mdina plateau, 185 metres above sea level, lies on a hill protected by steep cliffs to its east, north and north east. To its south west it is on the level of the high ground but isolated by a moat dug in the rock and crossed at two gates. The other entrance in Magazenes Street is just a "hole in the walls" constructed after 1890 for the benefit of the inhabitants when a railway station was built at Mtarfa. The bastion walls to the north, east and south are of Roman origin and vertical, those to the side of the main entrance are Saracenic with modifications and additions by the Grand Masters. Classical writers such as the Greek geographer Ptolemy, Mar-

cus Tullius Cicero, Livy and Diodorus Siculus refer to the city Melita and extol its rich architecture and its stately palaces.

Luke the Evangelist, who in Acts, chapters 28-29, describes in great detail the Pauline Shipwreck in A.D. 60, refers to the protos or chief-man of the Island Publius and his country villa not far from the site of the shipwreck.

Immemorial tradition also recalls his palace within the city, believed to be the site of the present Cathedral as well as the chief man's conversion to Christianity and consecration as a bishop.

During the Arab period Mdina was inhabited by a Moslem community with its cemetery just outside the town.

In 1090 Count Roger of Normandy raided the island and landed for a day. His own scribe and secretary the French monk Geoffroi Malaterra narrates how his small force overcame the feeble resistance of the inhabitants and how he advanced on the town of Mdina. The Qaid or Governor submitted, surrendered mules, horses, arms and money and swore according to his own religion that he would pay annual tribute. A painting of Count Roger's entry was commissioned in 1713 from the Maltese painter Alessio Erardi for the Cathedral Sacristy. But in 1127 the island was really conquered by Roger II. The Arabs were expelled definitively and completely in 1224.

Mdina increased in importance in the following centuries under the Swabians, Angevins, Aragonese and Castilians. Many of its mediaeval and so called "Siculo-Norman" buildings were erected in this period.

The Cathedral, whose dedication to St. Paul is already documented in 1299, was rebuilt, like so many other of the great churches of the period in Sicily and South Italy, in the Apulian-Romanesque style

with a compact facade with a single porch, a steeply pitched roof and a single free-standing belfry to the left. Two of the frescoes executed c. 1580 by Matteo Perez d'Aleccio for the Magisterial Palace in Valletta give the artist's impression of what it looked like. Mdina became the centre of the popular town council or autonomous commune, called Università, headed by the Hakem assisted by a body of Jurats. The Hakem was called Capitano della Verga or Captain of the Rod because a rod - the symbol of his office - was always carried by a page behind him. The Town Council or Università controlled the internal affairs of the island, imposed taxes and raised loans, appointed judges, supervised weights and measures and made representations to the King on behalf of the people.

Mdina was visited in 1355 by King Frederick III of Aragon and in 1432 by King Alfonso I of Sicily (V of Aragon).

The latter stayed for three months at Casa Inguanez revictualling his fleet after a successful expedition against Tunis. In 1447 this same King Alfonso ordered the arms of the Inguanez family to be affixed to the inside of the main gate at Mdina.

In 1427 King Alfonso gave to the Maltese their Magna Carta or Charter of Liberty in recognition of their ability to redeem their island from the rapacious Viceroy of Sicily Don Gonzales de Monroy - the Maltese had plundered his goods at Mdina and his wife at the Borgo Castle. In this document, still preserved in Malta's National Library, our islands are called Membrum Notabile of the Royal Crown. The appellative Notabile remained distinctive of Mdina, as Felix is distinctive of Palermo and Nobilis of Messina.

The old city was for several centuries the target of raids by pirates and corsairs who often landed on the unguarded coasts of our islands and plundered, pillaged and captured the islanders.

In 1429 Mdina was attacked by 18000 Saracens and its patron saint, the Apostle Paul, is said to have appeared riding on horseback and brandishing an enormous sword to raise the morale of the people.

The episode has been reproduced by several artists including Mattia Preti whose picture of the apparition is affixed in the Mdina Cathedral.

These frequent attacks naturally caused a depopulation of the city and the gradual decay of its houses. The Università made continuous efforts to remedy the situation and made representations to the king to order Mdina's townsmen to reside in the city. The kings and their representatives often refused to intervene.

The following is the text of a petition of 1410: "Whereas the said city of Malta is small and only partly inhabited, with numerous empty houses belonging to the townsmen of the said island who live and remain in the villages of the island ceasing to inhabit the said city... that it may please His Gracious Majesty to command and order that for the defence and protection of the said city, the Jurats and Council should have the authority and will to constrain the said townsmen to live and stay in the city (Cathedral Archives, Misc. 34). In 1524 Emperor Charles V of Spain offered Malta to the Order of St. John as its new home.

On 28 June 1524 Grand Master l'Isle Adam elected eight commissioners to spy the land. In their unenthusiastic report the commissioners referred to Mdina as an "old deserted town" on a hill seven miles inland. In 1536 however Jean Quentin d'Autun in his book published in Lyons (which is Malta's earliest printed description) describes Mdina as "quite pleasant and well looked after according to the tastes of the place and the people" (par. 12).

The Grand Masters after their election made their solemn entry into Mdina and had to swear to

maintain the privileges of the Università before receiving the symbolic keys of the city. One of the Jurats, in the words of G.P. Badger (Description of Malta and Gozo, 1838) addressed the Grand Master as follows: "Most Serene Lord, the Divine Majesty has been pleased to favour us and this city, by placing over us so great a prince as lord and master; and the high honour is conferred upon me of presenting to your serene Majesty the keys of this city in order that you may take possession thereof.

Therefore my colleagues and myself, in all humility beg of your most serene Highness to deign to swear upon the habit of the Grand Cross, that you will observe all the privileges, and franchises, and usages of this city, and of the island of Malta, which were conceded to them by the most serene Sovereigns of Aragon and Sicily...". The Grand Master then laid his hand upon the cross on his breast, and said: "I am bound to do so, I swear". After the keys were delivered into his hand, the procession proceeded to the Cathedral, and after the celebration of the Mass, the pageant terminated. A painting by Antoine Favray in the Valletta Palace depicts the solemn entry of the first Grand Master, l'Isle Adam, into Mdina and his receiving the symbolic keys. The old and wearied Grand Master incidentally, died four years later in Mdina.

The musical archives of the Cathedral contain musical scores composed for the solemn entry of a Grand Master into the Old City.

In 1551 the Muslim forces under the command of Sinam Pasha landed in Malta and attacked Mdina. During the great siege of 1565 the Turks made a last desperate attack to capture Mdina but were driven out. After the fall of St. Elmo the Knights hanged one

Turkish prisoner upon the walls of Mdina every morning. Mdina declined in status soon after the Knights constructed their new city, Valletta. Mdina became Città Vecchia, the Old City. The Order also whittled the powers of its Commune. Her defences were extensively repaired, between 1610 and 1616 and Grand Master Garzes granted privileges to its inhabitants to obstruct its further depopulation but some time later the unpopular Grand Master Lascaris (1636-1657) decided to dismantle its defences and arrested a

number of women of Mdina who attacked the Grand Master's men when the latter replaced the city's brass canons with inferior iron pieces.

In 1660 c. Grand Master De Redin added three polygonal bastions to Mdina's South wall: they are called Bastione San Pietro, Bastione del Palazzo and Bastione De Redin. The earthquake of 1693 destroyed most of Mdina's mediaeval and "Siculo-Norman" buildings, including the Cathedral with its works of art, except for the apse, newly constructed by

Side: panoramic view of the city with the dome of the Cathedral in the foreground.

Gafà and painted by Mattia Preti, and the Old Sacristy. The earthquake in turn caused another exodus of people from Mdina.

Grand Master Vilhena, who on his election found Mdina practically uninhabited, tried to inject new life by embarking on an extensive rebuilding programme. He reshaped the entrance, added to the fortifications, embellished the city gates and constructed a Magisterial Palace on the site of the old Town Council. This he did also to impress upon the people and the nobility the might of the princely institution he represented. His escutcheon is frequently repeated on the buildings, including the old Seminary, for which he also contributed funding.

In 1798, when Napoleon ousted the Knights, General Vaubois advanced on Mdina, and received the keys of the city from the city fathers who were unable to make effective resistance.

But when on 2 September 1798 the French attempted to auction objects belonging to the Carmelite Church, the people prevented them. Commander Masson was personally attacked and later hurled from a balcony in Rabat and killed. Mdina once more had played its part: the revolution spread and in 1800 the French surrendered.

In 1818 Sir Thomas Maitland abolished the powers of the Università completely and Mdina lost its centre of power and importance. But it retained and still retains its dignity, and its aristocratic and ecclesiastical atmosphere as the seat of the Bishopric and the Nobility.

Main Gate

The Main Gate to the City was erected in 1724 by Grand Master De Vilhena, replacing an earlier drawbridge gate the outline of which, now walled up, is still visible some metres away to the right of the present gate. It is reached by a narrow stone bridge, over a moat dug out by the Arabs, and decorated with stone trophies of arms supported by lions - the lion forms part of Grand Master Vilhena's escutcheon.

On the outside are a Latin inscription giving the date and some details of the new gate's erection, a trophy beautifully carved in stone and decorated with martial and triumphal symbols and with the Grand Master's arms on white marble, and on top the coat-of-arms of the city of Mdina and again that of Vilhena.

On the inside the Latin inscription commemorates Antonio Inguanez who in 1428 quelled a rebellion as well as his coat-of-arms.

Bas-relief carvings of stone recall the patron saints of the city: St. Paul, St. Publius and St. Agatha.

A Roman headless marble statue, now in the Museum of Roman Antiquities, was once encased in the wall of the main entrance.

The main entrance Gate to the city, erected in 1724 by the Grand Master of Vilhena.

Magisterial Palace

The Magisterial Palace, erected by Vilhena in about 1730, now converted to a Museum of Natural History, in St. Publius Square, replaces the Town Hall or Municipium of the local Government (the Università) which had been constructed c. 1454. Following the earthquake of 1693 Grand Master Vilhena took the opportunity not only to embellish the entrance but also to construct in the area his Magisterial Palace.

Palazzo Vilhena is entered through a screen wall with a heraldic gateway introducing an imposing open courtyard whose wings have a series of balconies on two floors. The real entrance is through a sculpted doorway with banded columns and with the effigy and coat-of-arms, on white marble, of the Grand Master.

Built to the design of architect De Mondion, the Palaces epitomize French Baroque architecture as introduced in Malta at the beginning of the 18th century.

One hall of the Palace, decorated with six escutcheons of holders of the office of Captain of the Rod from the time of Gregorio Bonnici Platamone, was retained as supreme court of the Town Council. Since the Middle Ages Malta enjoyed a popular Council, known as the Università; controlling the island's internal affairs, appointing judges and imposing taxes. In 1365 a royal statute instituted a body of officials on the lines of the principal self-governing communities of Sicily. Its head was the Capitano della Verga because a rod was the symbol of his office. His official residence was the Magisterial Palace; he was also granted a personal body guard and a group of officers quartered in the palace.

He presided over a body of locally erected giurati. When Grand Master Vilhena erected his palace, their seat of council was moved to a newly erected fine baroque palace in Villegaignon Street at the corner of Cathedral Square. The posts of Captain of the Rod and Jurats functioned until 1819 when they were abolished by Governor Sir Thomas Maitland.

In 1908 Palazzo Vilhena, trans-

formed into a hospital, was formally inaugurated by King Edward VII and named Connaught Hospital after the King's brother, the Duke of Connaught. The Hospital closed in 1956. On 22 June 1973 the building was reopened as the National Museum of Natural History. The Museum comprises nine sections, three of which are located on the first floor and display collections of Insects, Birds and Shells. The Halls on the Ground Floor contain the sections of Skeletal Anatomy, Fish, Geology, Fossils, Minerals and Animals. On the roof is a Cactus Garden and on the right of the courtyard entrance is an aquarium. The greater part of the exhibits are items of local origin. The display is highly instructive and detailed especially in the sections of geology and mineralogy.

Tower of the Standard

The 16th century tower with a rugged facade in St. Publius Square, known as Torre dello Stendardo or Tower of the Standard served as a watch-tower and guardian. It was lit with bonfires to warn the people of any landings by enemy troops. It replaces the earlier Torre Mastra.

The Corte Capitanale housed the Courts of Justice presided over by the Captain of the Rod. The sculpted figures of Justice and Mercy are placed on the exterior over the balcony, beneath the incised motto Legibus et Armis, By Laws and Arms.

Side: Tower of the Standard.

Photo above: National Museum of Natural History, one of whose new sections houses a collection of shells.

Cathedral Museum

The Cathedral Museum in Arch-bishop Square is an imposing baroque palace housing rich collections of art and archaeology as well as important archives.

The building, completed in 1744, was constructed as a Diocesan Seminary and served its purpose up to the first decade of the present century; it was then utilized by various ecclesiastical and educational institutions until on 5 January 1969 it was inaugurated by Sir Maurice Dorman, Governor-General of Malta, as the Cathedral's Museum. The main bulk of the art collections is a legacy by Count Saverio Marchese (1757-1833). The Count, a highly cultured art lover and patron of the arts, bequeathed all the paintings extant in his house at Valletta, except the family portraits, his old master drawings and his rare collection of invaluable prints to his nephew on condition that when his line became extinct they would be forwarded to the Cathedral. The condition was verified in 1896. The Marchese collection of prints included a substantial part of the collections of Count Francesco Seratti of Florence, later purchased by John Robert Steward and including a substantial number of woodcuts and copperplates by Albrecht Dürer and the early 16th cent. German School.

The spacious entrance, containing a bas-relief of Count Marchese and a Maltese clock with a perpetual calendar manufactured in 1888 by the renowned Michelangelo Saplano leads to the central high courtyard that gives light and air to the whole building. The glazed-in corridors round this courtyard contain various remains of the old Cathedral. A number of choir-stalls with inlaid panels representing saints who enjoyed popular devotion in 15th century Malta such as St. Catherine, St. Michael and St. Apollonia were originally

The Capitanale courtyard and the main entrance to the Cathedral Museum.

Catheral Museum: one of the rooms inside where several works of the collection are on dispaly.

Cathedral Museum: photo above, earthenware finds housed in one of the museum's rooms. Side page: important ceramic plate of the 16th century.

commissioned for the Dominican Priory of Rabat but were later ceded to the Cathedral. On the other side of the Corridor are remains of a richly carved and gilt balcony once decorating the organ loft: the mixture of sacred and profane elements in its decoration is typical of the Renaissance style.

In the innermost part of the corridor is a Parchment gallery with important documents of the Malta Commune, including an official copy of the Cession of Malta to Antonio da Cardona in 1420 and the Act of Ransom in 1441, Royal Privileges, Papal Bulls and Inquisitorial Documents.

A newly opened large room on the right of the entrance serves for the temporary display of new acquisitions but the room is also offered to local artists for exhibiting their latest works and holding one-man exhibitions.

The old refectory of the seminary has been preserved complete, with the original tables of 1744 (note their worn-out feet), the complete panelling covering the walls and the covered pulpit or seat for the lector reading during meals.

Behind the refectory is a small room with ceramics ranging from Phoenician to recent times. In 1983 the collection was enriched by Mr Roger Vella Bonavita's donation of Punic-Roman pieces from the Bonavita collection. Of special importance is a 16th cent. ceramic dish manufactured in Urbino and representing the biblical scene of Joshua stopping the sun.

Adjacent to this room but with an entrance from the corridor is the Mgr. Karm Psaila Room, a literary shrine with manuscripts, publications and personal memories of Malta's National poet, whose Innu Malti (Malta's national anthem) set to music by Mro. R. Samut is engraved in marble (lyrics and score) in a corner of the room.

The most important collection on display on the ground floor is certainly the Numismatic collection illustrating Malta's varied history, over a span of over two thousand years, through its coinage. The coins and medals are exhibited in such a way that one can see through a mirror both their obverse and their reverse at one and the same time. This vast collection was amassed from various donations by five private owners: the most important of these was Can. Isidoro

Formosa Montalto, whose scholarly collection included some rare specimens of Roman Imperial coinage.

Of special interest is the complete set of Roman coins of Ancient Malta and Gozo minted for our islands by the local municipia when the Maltese people were accorded by Rome the privileged status of socii. The section of the Order includes some rare specimens. The English coins date from William the Conqueror. The Papal section includes a medal of Pope Celestine V (1294).

The Museum's majestic staircase takes the visitor to a landing place, in a corner of which is an 18th cent. sedan-chair, leading to the Vestments' Hall, with a central balustraded balcony.

Apart from embroidered vestments with donors' coat-of-arms, illuminated codices on parchment and rare books are also exhibited. Amongst these is a second edition of King Henry VIII's Assertio Septem Sacramentorum for which he was given the title of Defensor Fidei, when the King rejected the doctrine of Martin Luther.

A reliquary with ivories, brought from Rhodes, should not be missed by the visitor.

The masterpiece of the Museum's picture-gallery is the St. Paul Polyptych which up to 1682 was the retable of the old Cathedral.

It was then replaced by Mattia Preti's canvas but the central part was also placed beneath the new altarpiece until 1780.

St. Paul, enthroned in majesty, with a sword in his right hand and a book in his left, is surrounded by various episodes of his life, including various ones with details of his Maltese Shipwreck in A.D. 60, an indication that the work was commissioned for Malta.

It has been attributed to the entourage of Luis Borrassa (died 1425 circa) of Catalunya and historically the date coincides with a modification in the edifice of the old church by the addition of a horizontal rectangular wing.

The predella includes St. Peter, St. Catherine of Alexandria and St. Agatha (secondary patroness of Malta and patroness of Sicily). The Spanish origin of the Polyptych links well with two nearby panels of the Valencian School representing St. John the Baptist and the Dormition of the Virgin. They also date from the 15th century. Equally important are the two remaining parts of another polyptych commissioned for St. Peter's Nunnery, Mdina showing St. Peter (originally on panel) and a predella (on panel) with Christ, St. Paul and the Apostles. Beneath is an inscription: Magister Salvu de Antoni Messanensis me pinxit 1510. St. Agatha is again represented by a panel with the effigy and date of the donor, Don Giuseppe Manduca. The Scourging of Christ by Palma il Giovane (1540-1628), two companion pictures on copper, The Baptist and St. Jerome and a tryptych of Flemish origin representing the Deposition as well as a canvas of Our Lady of the Rosary, from a rural chapel in Siggiewi, inscribed Gio Maria Habela and dated 1591 are other paintings of interest.

The latter is one of the earliest documented works by a Maltese artist. Expulsion from Eden by Bernardo Strozzi (1581-1644) (at the back of St. Paul's Polyptych) is a fine original, in the Caravaggesque style, which has been repeated elsewhere by the master. A panel of the old Umbrian School represents St. Catherine of Siena, whereas 4 canvases by Frans Mostaert (mid 16th cent.) illustrate the Parable of the Good Samaritan.

Works by artists active in the 19th cent. in Malta are on display in a small room near the centre of the large hall. The two Grand Harbour Views signed by Anton Schranz and dated 1818 were commissioned by Count Saverio Marchese for a total of 120 scudi.

The masterpiece in the Museum's picture gallery is the polyptych of Saint Paul which until 1682 was the altar-piece in the ancient Cathedral. Subsequently, it was replaced with a canvas by Mattia Preti but the central part was left beneath the new altar-piece until 1780.

Details of the polyptych of Saint Paul, representig above, Saint Paul together with Saint Catherine of Alexandria and Saint Agatha, the second patron sain of Malta. Below: St. Paul's shipwreck which took place in Malta in 60 A.D..

Side: a panel of the old Umbrian school depicting Saint Catherine of Siena.

Below: the expulsion from Eden by Bernardo Strozzi (1581-1644).

Side page: the works shown here are signed by Anton Schranz and represent two views of Porto Grande.

The octagonal chapel is a jewel of 18th cent. art and a museum in miniature. In 1745, just one year after the completion of the building, Bishop Alpheran contracted with Maestro Claudio Durante for a marble altar and later for the marble pavement with 704 quadrelli. In 1749 he commissioned from Favray altar-piece of the Annunciation, signed and dated 1749 and the four ovals representing the Saints Peter, Paul, Charles Borromeo and Francis Sales. The oval beneath the altarpiece was commissioned from the Maltese contemporary and able artist Francesco Zahra (1710-1773) along with the elliptical St. Paul with a vignette of Mdina and the Portrait of G. Master Antonio De Vilhena in the nearby hall which served as an extension to the Chapel. The inlaid cabinet in the corner contains a Byzantine altarstone with enamels and a metal Romanesque chalice.

Photo below: the marble altar commissioned by Bischop Alpheran (1745).

Cathedral Church

According to tradition Malta's earliest Cathedral was dedicated to the Blessed Virgin, Mother of God, dilapidated in the Muslim period and reconstructed and rededicated to St. Paul after the Norman conquest.

This old church was modified and enlarged several times. In 1419 a horizontal rectangular wing was added to the edifice; in 1626 Bishop Baldassare Cagliares added a recess at the back and in 1679 Bishop Molina laid the first stone of the choir which was inaugurated on 28 June 1682. The terrible earthquake of 11 January 1693 destroyed the old Cathedral almost completely except for the sacristy and the newly constructed choir. The latter had already been decorated with a fine altarpiece, a canvas representing St. Paul's Conversion and a fresco depicting St. Paul's Shipwreck as well as five other canvases, all painted by Mattia Preti (1613-1699). These fortunately survived the earthquake.

The reconstruction of a larger Cathedral in the new baroque style was immediately taken in hand and entrusted to the Maltese architect Lorenzo Gafà who eleven years before had constructed the apsed choir. There was no need for a new plan: Gafà had previously submitted the plan and wooden model for a church in the new baroque style and the Cathedral Chapter had examined and approved them on 18 May 1692, that is eight months before the earthquake had taken place. The new Cathedral was com-

pleted and consecrated in October 1702 by Bishop Cocco Palmieri (1684-1713) whose coat-of-arms along with those of the reigning Grand Master Fra Ramon Perellos (1697-1720) and of the City of Mdina were placed on the facade over the main entrance.

All the side altars were painted by followers of Mattia Preti. Those on the right aisle represent the Martyrdom of St. Publius, St. Cajetan and St. Luke; those on the left were substituted by other representations of the same subjects by 19th century Italian artists on the initiative of Can. Paolo Pullicino. Francesco Grandi (1831-1891) painted the Pentecost, Pietro Gagliardi (1809-1890) painted The Madonna as the Patroness of Malta with a view of the Grand Harbour and Domenico Bruschi (1840-1910) depicted the Annunciation.

The Cathedral is enriched by three marble statues by Giuseppe Valenti of Palermo representing St. Publius on the right of the entrance and the Evangelists St. Luke and St. John in the Chancel as lecterns.

The Church has four monuments dedicated to four Maltese Prelates - Bishop Francesco Saverio Caruana, (erected in marble in 1838), Bishop Publius Maria Sant (by Mario Gori in marble, 1874), Cardinal Fabrizio Sceberras Testaferrata, Bishop of Senegallia and Malta's only Cardinal, and the life-size monument in bronze to Mgr. Sir Michael Gonzi, Malta's first Metropolitan Archbishop, executed by Vincent Apap in 1971.

The painting in the Cupola, replacing earlier paintings by Manno and Gallucci both ruined by damage caused on the outside wall through inclement weather, was executed by Mario Caffaro Rore of Turin in 1955. St. Peter and St. Paul, flanked by a host of saints, including Malta's secondary patrons, Publius and Agatha, are presented by Christ to the Almighty Father. The scene recalls Christ's words: He who testifies to me before men, I will testify to him before my Father.

The dome, constructed by Lorenzo Gafà, is perhaps the most spectacu-

lar in Malta. The vault was painted in fresco by the Sicilian brothers, Antonio and Vincenzo Manno in 1794. The central pieces represent Triumph over Heresy (choir) and various Episodes from St. Paul's Life (nave and transepts). The two enclosed chapels on the side of the chancel have fine paintings by Francesco Zahra (1710-1773) in their domes, pendentives and lunettes. Both have fine inlaid marble pavements executed by Mro. Claudio Durante and wooden carved and gilt gates by Francesco Zahra. The Chapel of the Blessed Sacrament has an old (15th cent.) icon of the Virgin and an exquisite silver tabernacle by Benvenuto Cellini of the 19th cent., a descendant of the famous 16th cent. goldsmith. The Chapel of the Cross has three carved 17th cent. statues, the Crucifix (attr.to Fra Innocenzo da Petralia) donated in 1648, flanked by the Virgin and St. John.

On this page: the interior and exterior of the dome of the Cathedral. Side page: the interior of the Cathedral.

Falzon Palace

(Norman House)

One of the best preserved buildings is Palazzo Falzon. Initially constructed, c. 1495, by the Aragonese Vice-Admiral Falzon but modified by many alterations and additions, it was acquired by Capt. Olaf Gollcher, a collector with fine taste who left it in trust as a Museum. Grand Master L'Isle Adam is said to have stayed in it during his first state visit in 1530. It is popularly known as the "Norman" House but the term is misleading and refers in a wider sense to any mediaeval building anteceding the coming of the Knights in 1530.

The Museum, open only on certain days, contains paintings, old furniture, armour, a fine collection of carpets, and various other items decorating the bedroom, dining room, landing and other rooms.

The graceful double windows with slender colonettes, characteristic of Maltese late medieval architecture, are admired in this and other palaces, such as S. Sofia, Gatto Murina and those in Magazenes Street and St. Peter's Street.

Greeks' Gate

Greeks' Square in the south western part of the city is said to have been inhabited by a Greek colony, perhaps reminiscent of the Byzantine period.

The church in its corner (constructed 1550, rebuilt 1692) is dedicated to St. Nicholas, a Greek Saint.

Greeks' Gate leading to the ditch by a steep slope is the second main gate, also embellished by Grand Master Vilhena in 1725 and decorated with commemorative inscriptions, the Vilhena coat-of-arms and an effigy of the city's patron, St. Paul.

Villegaignon Street

Villegaignon Street, dividing the old City into two, East and West, is so named after the Knight who organized the defence of Mdina against the Turks in 1551. Along its length lie various Chapels and stately Patrician Houses.

The Churches are St. Agatha and St. Peter's at the entrance and Our Lady of Light and the Carmelite Priory at the far end of the road. St. Peter's, adorned with an altar-piece by Mattia Preti (1613-1699) is adjoined to a nunnery of cloistered nuns of the Order of St. Benedict. The elliptical church of the Carmelite

Friars is enriched with a fine canvas of the Annunciation by Stefano Erardi (1630-1716).

The Maltese revolt against the French started when the French ransacked this church in 1798. Among the most conspicuous palaces are Palazzo Inguanez at the entrance, seat of the most ancient titled family (Barons of Bucana since 1350), Casa Testaferrata (seat of the Marquis of St. Vincent Ferreri, created 1716), the Banca Giuratale, now being transformed into a Public Records Office, and Palazzo S. Sofia, the ground floor of which is perhaps the oldest extant building in Mdina.

Via Villegaignon.

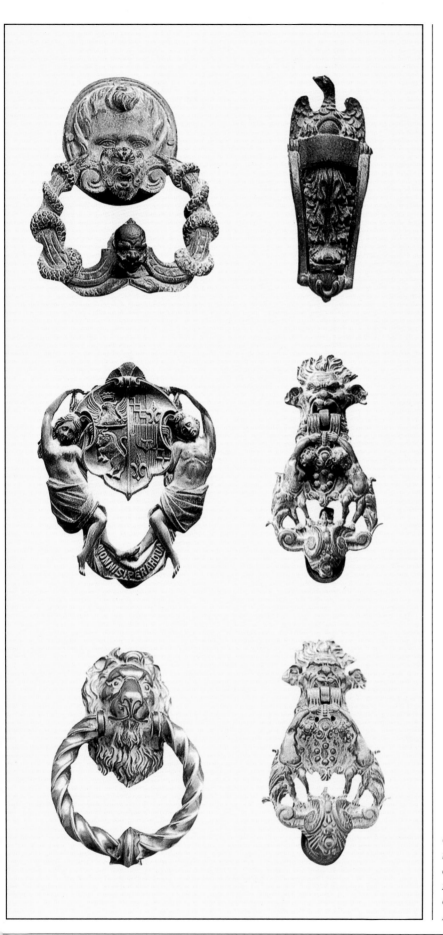

One of the attractions of Malta is to be found in the numerous door-knockers, some old, some more modern, which can be seen on the doors of the buildings and houses in the city.

Rabat

Both Rabat and Mdina are perched on a ridge dominating the whole expanse of the island and of the sea beyond. Both have been a centre of habitation for thousands of years.

Rabat incorporates a good part of the old Roman city which was reduced to its present outline by the Arabs.

This explains how the sumptuous townhouse with its fine polychrome mosaic pavements once inside the Roman town Melita now forms part of Rabat as the Museum of Roman Antiquities.

In the Roman era the Melita area was enriched with palaces and temples, relics of which are the inscriptions, columns, capitals and mosaics in the Museum of Roman Antiquities.

The Rabat area is intimately connected with the introduction of Christianity in our Islands: in A.D. 60 St. Paul the Apostle, under arrest on his way to Rome and shipwrecked on our shores, is said to have lived or slept for three months in a cave within the ditch outside the walls of the old Roman city - St. Paul's Grotto - using it as a centre for his activity in establishing a primitive Christian community.

This place has always been dedicated to St. Paul - with an overstanding church and an important cemetery around it in the mediaeval period.

Burial being prohibited inside the walls of the city, the area outside the ditch, from St. Paul's Grotto to Buskett, abounds with a concentration of hypogea - or burial places - of pagan, Jewish or Christian origin dug in live rock by the Phoenicians, Greeks, Romans and Byzantines. Their tombs contain a rich variety of architectural elements. The largest of these are the St. Paul's and the St. Agatha's complex in the Hal-Bajjada district.

Before the coming of the Knights, Rabat became the centre of various religious Orders who preferred to erect their houses in a place not far from the capital city but also sufficiently secluded for their monastic recollection. The Knights, concentrated in Vittoriosa and Valletta, erected very few constructions in Rabat and did little to embellish the area. Today besides schools and colleges, Rabat has various social and band clubs, a market which is very popular on Sunday mornings and playing fields.

The Rabat area is ideal for walks in the countryside.

Museum of Roman Antiquities

The misnamed Roman "villa" Museum covers the site of a rich and sumptuously decorated town house belonging to a wealthy person in Roman Malta. The site, discovered in 1881 and further excavated in 1920-24, contains a number of remarkably fine mosaic polychrome pavements and some original architectural elements. A number of rooms were constructed to protect the mosaics and an upper hall was added to provide exhibition space and a suitable entrance. The porticoed neo-classical facade was completed in 1925.

The main attraction are the mosaics, rated among the finest and oldest from the West Mediterranean and compare with those of Sicily and Pompeii. Originally these mosaics paved the peristyle, once supported by 16 columns and two adjacent rooms. One of the pavements has only survived poorly in patches; the other rooms are characterized by an illusion of three dimensional depth.

Partial views of the numerous archaeological finds, mainly of the Roman age, collected together in the museum.

The interior of the Church of Saint Paul.

St. Paul's Collegiate Church

St. Paul's Collegiate Church is constructed upon, but to the left of St. Paul's Grotto, just outside the walls and in the ditch of the old city, hence its mention in old documents as St. Paul Outside The Walls.

The earliest documentary evidence referring to it dates from 1372. A Mediaeval cemetery with many private chapels and memorials flourished on the left of the Church.

The dedication to St. Paul is due to the immemorial tradition of St. Paul's use of the cave as a base for his preaching and building of an incipient Christian community during his three months' stay in Malta in A.D. 60. For this reason St. Paul's Grotto was described by the Cathedral Chapter as "the foundation stone of the Church in Malta".

Early in the 17th century, a Spanish nobleman from Cordova, Juan Beneguas, reactivated devotion and rendered the place a centre of popular cult and of pilgrimages by local and foreign visitors.

In 1609 he succeeded in severing St. Paul's Grotto from the overstanding Parish Church and in 1619 ceded it to the Grandmaster and his Order. Grand Master Alof de Wignacourt soon transformed it into a Collegiate of the Order, constructed a college of chaplains officiating the new institution and erected a Collegio as well as a new church of St. Publius, adjacent to St. Paul's Parish Church.

The Order of St. John enriched the place with various works of art, including a fine altarpiece of St. Publius by Mattia Preti, an altarpiece of the Eucharist by Francesco Zahra (1710-1773), a statue of St. Paul over his altar in the Grotto executed by the Maltese sculptor Melchiorre Gafà though completed by his master Ercole Ferrata, following Gafà's death, precious silverplate and a fine 18th cent. Neapolitan organ by Giuseppe del Piano. Among its works of art are

three paintings by Stefano Erardi (1630-1716), namely St. Anne, the huge altar-piece representing St. Paul's Shipwreck and the over-standing lunette depicting the Apotheosis of St. Paul. Perhaps the best work is Francesco Zahra's altar-piece of the Holy Family for a side altar. From Preti's workshop are The Stoning of St. Stephen in the transept and St. Michael as well as the oval depicting God the Father in the chapel on the right of the entrance. The titular statue, imitating that by Gafà in Valletta, was carved by Giovanni Caruana in 1774. The vault and dome were painted by the Brescian Elio Coccoli during this century.

Photo below: Neapolitan organ of the 18th century, the work of Giuseppe del Piano.

St. Paul's Grotto

The inner cave of the underground cave was endowed with a new marble statue, executed in Rome and attributed to the School of Bernini, donated by Grand Master Pinto in 1743. The silver lamp-stand in the form of a galley was donated by Grand Master de Moyana in 1960 whereas the four bronze lampstands on the floor were acquired from the spoils of the late Pope Paul VI.

STOLO MELITENSIÙ
SIUM PATRONO
PINTUS MELITÆ
OS PRINCEPS
D. D.

27 TA MEJJU 1990
-GROTTA MQADDSA
APA ĠWANNI PAWLU II
NES L-ISTATWA TA' S.PAWL

Museum of St. Paul's Church

The Collegio (Wignacourt College) was converted to a Museum in 1981. Access is either from the main door or else from an underground passage hewn in the rock in 1683 and linking the former residence of the officiating clergy with their church. A spacious arched corridor flanked by rooms on one side and a large garden on the other forms the ground floor, and also leads to the Rector's Quarters and Garden extending over a complex of catacombs once opened for visitors, the most important of whom was Lord Nelson on 4 May 1800. The main floor contains precious works of art, including a picture gallery, a collection of Punic-Roman pottery dating from 600 B.C. to 200 A.D., coins, old maps and rare books, old furniture including a galley's altar, sculptures, and portraits located in the Chapter Hall, the Treasurer's Room, the small baroque chapel, various other rooms and the wide spacious corridor. Three rooms still retain the planks of the original roofing. The collection includes many works by Maltese artists or foreign artists active in Malta.

St. Paul's Catacombs

The underground area from St. Paul's Grotto to Buskett is a catacombal area characterized by many family hypogea, or burial places, of Punic, Roman, Jewish or Christian origin. This is easily explained by the fact that burial was prohibited inside the city. The Maltese catacombs are extremely rich in architecture though poor in art and epigraphy. They were hewn in live-rock as simple family burial places, very close to one another and sometimes they have been extended to form one complex.

By far the largest of these complexes are the St. Paul's catacombs in Hal-Bajjada Street. They also contain a variety of types of graves as well as a few frescoes with inscriptions, including the name of a certain Eutychion. A steep flight of steps cut in live rock (underneath the present staircase of recent construction) leads to the chapel and main hall with an agape table at each end. Various passages lead the visitor into a labyrinth of narrow galleries forming several storeys.

St. Agatha's Church

Close to the Parish Church, is a small church, which is dedicated to St. Agatha, a young Sicilian saint. Together with this Church there is a renowned underground Crypt, St. Agatha's Catacombs, and the Convent of the Missionary Society of St. Paul founded by Monsignor Joseph De Piro in 1933 and the Archaeological Museum which is housed in the same convent.

From the earliest days of the foundation of the Society, the Museum had always been at heart to the founder and members of the Society. Monsignor De Piro was a keen collector of archaeological items, especially pottery which forms the greatest section in the Museum. A great variety of pottery, mostly of the 4th/3rd century B.C. is on show along the main Hall. Of special interest are the three tymiatheria made of local stone 6th century B.C. and a white marble torso of Aphrodite 300 B.C. which was found in Rabat.

In another Hall is exhibited a unique medieval collection of stone votive slabs which once formed a frieze in St. Agatha's Church which was built in 1504 A.D. Coins of those who ruled over Malta since the times of the Phoenicians, and a collection of paintings are also found here.

Adjacent to this Hall are found Church decorations which still decorate the old Church on feast day feast days. Of great interest is the alabaster statue of St. Agatha which is the main attraction in this section. It was brought from Trapani and was kept in the Crypt on the Main Altar since 1666, but now it is kept in the Museum. Different sizes of candlesticks, angels and flower vases, all sculpted in wood and gilded, are kept in showcases. Late medieval vessels used for wine and water during Mass service, and a collection of chalices and old Reliquaries, together with a fine Reliquary of Saint Agatha sculpted in wood in 1728, adorn this section.

The Hall on the first floor of the Museum is reserved for a crystal and mineral collection. This collection has been recently acquired from a benefactor of the Society, Mr. Fred Magri who is a Maltese living in Australia. It is of great importance as some of the crystals are very rare specimens. Local fossils, recently found in St. Agatha's grounds, are conserved in the same Hall.

A great variety of fossils which were found locally, and prehistoric remains of elephantmelitensis, hip-

popotami, deer and other animals are exhibited on the ground floor of this Museum.

Although small and privately owned, the Museum is opened daily to the public as many of the items exhibited are of great interest both to those who are interested in Maltese History and to the visitors who call at St. Agatha's complex.

Strong local tradition holds that the young lady, Agatha, crossed to Malta to seek refuge during the persecution of the Emperor Decius whose reign over the Roman Empire was from 249-251 A.D.. She hailed from Catania and as found in the history of her life, she was asked by the Catanese governor Quintilianus to be his wife. She refused his hand on several occasions and Quintilianus was angered by her attitude. Finally it was reported that she kept the Christian faith and for this reason she was tortured until her life expired on the 5th of February 251 A.D..

Of great interest are the frescoes which decorate this sacred place. Within the Crypt, one can see the three different ages when the fescoes were made. The earliest frescoes can be seen underneath, to the left hand side on entering the Crypt. Designs and decorations together with inscriptions, one in Greek and another in Latin, have been recently discovered as these were covered with plaster. These frescoes probably belong to the 4th/5th century A.D.. There are three frescoes, one showing a saint, probably representing St. Paul, another a Madonna and a third one is a bust of the Madonna suckling the Baby Jesus. These are in Byzantine style and they date back to the 12th century A.D.. The majority of frescoes which are twenty-nine in all, go back to 1480 A.D. and are attributed to Salvatore d'Antonio who spent some years on the Island c. 1470-1482 A.D..

Most of the pictures show Saint Agatha in different postures. Others show a bishop saint who is probably Publius, the Chief of Malta who was converted to Christianity by St. Paul. Some others show St. Leo-

nard, St. Blaise, St. Anthony of Egypt, St. Margaret of Antioch, St. Lucy, St. Venera, the Madonna with the Infant Jesus and the Madonna of Succour.

The main altar of the Crypt was made in 1666 A.D.. It replaced another altar which was cut in rock cfr. Comm. G.F. Abela "Della Descrizione di Malta" 1647 p. 43.

The present statue was donated by the Maltese sculptor Antoine Agius 1984. A side altar is dedicated to the Madonna, with the title of "Mater Divinae Gratiae", whose statue is made in terracotta. Nearby is a bust made of local stone showing St. Lucy with her hands joined together in a praying attitude. Two narrow passages from the Crypt lead to a vast Christian Catacomb renowned mostly for its unique frescoes, the various kinds of tombs and agape-tables and for its antiquity.

Opposite page: Saint Agatha. Fresco attributed to Salvatore d'Antonio (circa 1480) showing the coat of arms of the donor: the Bordino family. It has recently been restored by a Maltese artist.

On this page: one of the figures shows a saint, probably Saint Paul, whilst the other represents a woman with a child at her feet begging for grace.

Verdala

Verdala Palace at Buskett, designed in 1586 by the Maltese Girolamo Cassar (the architect of St. John's Co-Cathedral) was constructed by Grand Master Cardinal Hughes Loubens de Verdalle as a country villa with gardens.

The green wooded area around is called Buskett from the Italian Boschetto, small forest.

The basement is surrounded by a moat whereas a flight of steps across the ditch leads to the ground floor whose large vaulted hall is decorated with frescoes illustrating the Grand Master's achievements.

A beautiful elliptical staircase leads to the main floor.

The Chapel with a canvas by Preti is dedicated to St. Anthony the Abbot.

Panoramic view of the Palazzo Verdala by the Maltese designer Girolamo Cassar (1586).

Dingli

Nearby Dingli is a small pleasant village located near the highest point of the island with Dingli cliffs dropping 800 feet into the sea. The lonely chapel perched on the cliff's edge is dedicated to St. Mary Magdalene whereas the Parish Church is dedicated to Our Lady's Assumption.

Mosta

Mosta, so near to the Ta' Qali military aerodrome, was heavily bombed during the war but the church was providentially saved, even though a bomb penetrated the huge dome, hit the interior wall and rolled on the floor - no one was killed.

Designed in the grand neo-classical style by the Maltese architect Giorgio Grognet de Vasse' (1774-1862) and constructed by the master-mason Anglu Gatt, the church was completed in 1863 (and consecrated in 1871) with abundant voluntary help provided by the people. The new church was built around the old one and no scaffolding was used.

The magnificent dome - 37.34 metres in diameter - is the third largest in Europe and can accommodate about 10,000 people. It imitates the design of the Pantheon in Rome. The impression of space is moreover heightened by the frescoes by Giuseppe Cali (1846-1930). The church is beautifully decorated and illuminated on the titular feast-day, Our Lady's Assumption, on August 15.